MW01633963

## Welcoming New Christians
*A Guide For The Christian Initiation of Adults*
Scottdale, Penna.: Faith and Life, 1995
**With Jane Hoober Peifer**

## The Serving Leader
*5 Powerful Actions That Will Transform Your Team,*
*Your Business and Your Community*
San Francisco: Berrett-Koehler, 2003
**With Ken Jennings**

## Ten Thousand Horses
*How Leaders Harness Raw Potential*
*For Extraordinary Results*
San Francisco: Berrett-Koehler, 2007
**With Ken Jennings**

# With

John Stahl-Wert

Pittsburgh, PA

For Samuel Clair Hepner, 1916 - 2005

Go with God.

# Acknowledgements

This book was stirring around in my soul for several years before I took a week-long hermit's retreat in early 2004, pinning myself inside an eight-by-ten-foot cottage on a snow-swept mountainside in Washington, Pa. Thanks goes to my life companion Milonica for urging (insisting) that I slip away from the burdens of my work to think and to write. Chapter one and half of chapter two rolled out of my pen that week.

A special thanks to my mother, Mary Fianna Hepner Wert, for telling me the stories first, the ones I would later hear from many of her siblings. What would we do without stories? And what would we do if we could not laugh?  My mother has always asked these questions.

Phil Greene and Josh Colbert joined me at just the right time. Thank you for your artistry and professionalism, Phil, and for your entrepreneurial drive and your discipline, Josh. You and your company, Expanding Minds Creatives, have made the work of this publishing project a true pleasure.

Countless readers and listeners expressed their delight in the stories as they were being written; I am sorry that you are too many to name. My own wife, daughters, brothers, sisters, parents and my Uncle Sam heard sections read aloud, as did the editorial staff and authors of Berrett-Koehler Publishers, my church friends at Pittsburgh Mennonite, and, too, my friends Lisa Slayton and Rick Wellock one memorable evening at Chautauqua. Your enjoyment of these tales means more to me than I can say.

*Acknowledgements continued...*

Thanks to David Garber for the thorough editing assistance, and to Douglas Wilson, Ray Betler, and Nancy Engle for your typographical "catches."

And thank you, cousin Ken Hepner, for giving this book a final family read. Your words of blessing will never be forgotten.

Coming full circle, a second thanks to Milonica for pressing me to return to this book when, part way done, it fell by the wayside. Your unwavering encouragement for me to stop what I'm doing and write—you've done it again and again these nearly-thirty years of our marriage—is a treasure of inestimable worth.

My greatest appreciation goes to God who selected the Hepner family to be my family; and I extent my fondest love to this blessed family, too. Any living aunt or uncle, cousin, or innocent bystander (with eyebrows raised) will attest that a Hepner is not a quiet or uninteresting person! If there's a family that has made more noise than the Hepners, laughed more, charged forth more energetically, felt more deeply, or proven more definitively that God shows his power through weakness, I haven't met it. Any Hepner alive is invited to say with me, "The lines are fallen unto me in pleasant places; yea, I have a goodly heritage" (Psalms 16:6, KJV).

The word of the LORD came to me: "Son of man, take two sticks of wood and tie them together into one stick so that they will become one in your hand. And when the children of your people ask you what you mean by this, say to them, 'Thus says the Lord: I will take the Israelites out of the nations and make them one nation in the land. They will be my people, I will be their God, and my dwelling place will be with them.'"

**The Prophet Ezekiel
Ezekiel 37 KJV alt.**


The virgin will be with child and will give birth to a son, and they will call him Immanuel—which means, God with us.

**An Angel of the Lord
Matthew 1 NIV**


Priest:        The Lord be with you.
All:           And also with you.

**Eucharistic Prayer
The Order of Mass**


All authority has been given to me in heaven and on earth. Go therefore and make disciples of all the nations, baptizing them in the name of the Father and of the Son and of the Holy Spirit, teaching them to observe all things that I have commanded you; and lo, I am with you always, even to the end of the age.

**Jesus the Christ
Matthew 28 NKJV**

x

x

# Contents

# Chapter 1: Sam *With* Me

$A$t the exquisitely tender age of six, I was left for a few hours one day in the care of my mother's eldest brother, Samuel. I knew my Uncle Sam, though not well. My times of relating with him were meted out, like rationed candy, through the periodic trips my parents made "up home," piling my four older siblings and me into the 1961 Rambler for the several hours drive.

Samuel was a veteran of the Second World War, which caused me, child that I was of the Mennonites, to regard him with a certain measure of mystery and even trepidation. War was, after all, a very bad thing to get oneself mixed up in. Sam was also a bachelor, which in his case lent him panache and nobility. Eight years my mother's elder, he was dashing, charismatic, fun loving, and especially kind and companionable to the smallest of his many nephews and nieces.

I learned much later, in my own adult conversations with Sam, that his affinity for children was born of a lifelong painful yearning to be a daddy himself. A quick marriage to a worldly town girl just weeks before he shipped off to war turned into a divorce on the eve of his return. She thought he'd be killed and had received him into her faithless bed in the hopes of a military pension. Like the taking up of arms, the remarriage of a divorced man was forbidden by Sam's church. There were no exceptions. And so at the end of the war, he penitentially laid down his uniform and gave his life over to the children of others and to the unremitting ordeal of lonely pain-racked nights.

That day Sam took me on a ride to town in his horse-drawn carriage. His team of two great quarter horses pulled us at a clip that felt to me like flight, and at one point he even "let me hold the strings," as I later reported to my mother. What exhilaration to sit beside my tall, self-possessed uncle, separated from the brothers and sisters and throngs of cousins who always dwarfed my significance by their greater age and size. How wonderful to *be* someone, to be distinct, and to be known— all the result of a special time that my uncle had set aside to be with me.

When we got back to the house and to whatever family gathering had occasioned this particular visit, I tried to stick by my Uncle Sam. I didn't want to lose the feeling I had when it was just the two of us.

The day had been hot, and Sam's kitchen was full of people and noise. Other children's hands reached out for Sam the moment we came in the door, and adults called out for him to join their conversations. Dejectedly, I took one of the hard chairs lined up along the perimeter of the wall, resigned to the fact that my special time with Sam was over.

But I was wrong. Sam the onetime soldier, Sam the divorcee, had picked up a few additional worldly peccadilloes while away at war, one of which he wanted to share with me. Uncle Sam liked Coca-Cola, which he knew I had never tasted.

"I saw a movie one time, Johnny boy," Sam said. He spoke to me from across the room, his big voice and twinkling eyes pulling all the heads in his direction. Movies were also on the list of things not to do, it should just be noted. "And there was this bank robber, see, played by Jimmy Cagney, who didn't want to make his next heist alone."

The women in prayer veils and men in plain coats stopped talking altogether. Bank robbers and movie stars weren't discussed in this company. 'Heist' wasn't a word that called for too much usage, either.

"So Cagney says to this friend of his, Johnny, this friend he'd met in the hoosegow, he says, 'Are ya wit' me, babe?' And his friend says back to him, he says, 'I'm wit' cha!'

"So are ya wit' me, babe?" my Uncle Sam repeated, this time holding up a sparkling glass bottle of Coca-Cola he had just retrieved from the refrigerator. It was going to be just him and me after all. Bad guys pulling a heist of our own. Coke drinkers. Old friends from the hoosegow.

"I'm wit' cha!" I replied loudly, my ears burning red, my heart so very glad.

We drank our Coca-Colas together, Sam with me, me with Sam. And how wonderful that effervescent, burning elixir tasted on my happy tongue. How wonderful it tasted, being the boy with Uncle Sam.

*With* is a very powerful word. It may be the most powerful word. It's such a powerful word because it puts a spotlight on the matter of life's chief question: Who are you with? Who's with you?

The little preposition *With* carries the unchanging secret of the universe inside its four awkward letters. It causes our beginning, frames our being, occasions all that we learn, and provides the only meaning available to our end.

---

*Of* and *From* are also big words, revealing the long and sturdy cord that faithfully ties our distant point of origin right up to today. And so are *For* and *To*, pointing with hopeful fingers toward a destiny that lies far beyond the horizon line that we can currently see. But these prepositions are not nearly as big, not nearly as significant, as *With*.

*By* and *On* and *Through* and *In* and *Out* and *Back* and *Forth* and *Over* and *Under* and *Around* and *Beside* and *Before* and *Behind* and *Against* and *Between*—all play their smaller roles in the assemblage of our lives and activities. But in relation to *With*, they are merely a surrounding constellation, inaccurate points of dim reference, approximations of the greater truth they exist to serve.

When heaven and earth shall pass away, when all dimensions of time and space dissolve to reveal the life and truth to which they point, the only prepositions that will remain are *Of* and *For* and *With,* and the greatest of these is *With*! Who are you with? Who is with you?

That day my Uncle Samuel asked me the most important question I've ever been asked, and the most delightful. I'd like to pass on the favor. So why don't you head to the fridge or the coffeepot or the teakettle and set yourself up with a nice companionable beverage? Let's take a ride together, shall we? Pull a little heist. Share some time in the hoosegow. Are ya wit' me?

# Chapter 2: God *With* God

Grandpa Hepner liked to laugh. He also liked to tell stories, all kinds of stories, especially stories that made him laugh. In fact, I cannot recall hearing of any story attributed to Grandpa that *didn't* end with hilarity.

I know there were horrible stories in his past. I know he lived through terrible times. But his retelling of those old tales always made room for humor. I'm sure that the actual experiences would have been too painful to tell, too painful to endure, without a chance to "laugh real good," as he liked to say.

Food was scarce in Grandpa's childhood, but having no food was just a symptom of his true deprivation. There wasn't enough love in his home. And there wasn't enough laughter. Great-Grandpa was a drunk. Far worse, he had no sense of humor. A good night for my Grandpa was when his Dad was too drunk to find his way home. A bad night was when his frantic mother dragged him into the dark of the woods where they'd hide in a ditch and pray not to be found, pray that old Solomon would soon pass out and drop the butcher knife he was wielding. Grandpa lived through many bad nights.

Economic hardship followed Grandpa into his own adulthood. But Grandpa was not poor. The bond of love he forged with young, shy Sally Snyder endured through the births of eleven children, several miscarriages, the Great Depression, and years of back-breaking labor. This love endured to his final breath at age eighty-five, and burned on within her own heart until she died at ninety-two.

"Hoo-rah, Sally!" the young husband would bellow, his voice carrying the final two hundred yards to the house as he trudged home each day to be with his beloved. And Sally, modest sensible Sally, would nervously smooth down the wrinkles along the length of her full, tattered apron, blush around the ears, and await the gale-force of joy about to burst in upon her. A Mennonite upbringing did not prepare Sally to easily join such revelry. Often enough, she tried to shush her husband, tone him down. But against all of her own mother's pleadings she had married this unbeliever, this son of a drunk, and she truly did love him.

"I don't need nothin' but love!" Grandpa later liked to say, at which point Sally would redouble her focused labors over the old cookstove, embarrassed and maybe also pleased to have to hear about it all over again. Numbers of my uncles and aunts have repeatedly recounted this particular story from their childhood. Uncle Sam has told it to me, as have Gladys, Ruth, Dick, Jim, and my own mother, Mary. The whole brood, in fact, has inherited their father's love of a well-repeated story.

"No, nothin' but love. Why, send me out in the morning on a full breakfast well loved, and I can go the rest of the day on that alone." A brief pause goes here, well timed. "Long as I have a nice sandwich in my pocket to hold me to dinner."

Jack Benny and George Burns, working their beats in smoky nightclubs across America, the quick one-two of the snare set punctuat-

　　　　　　　　　　　　　　　　　　　　*With: A True Story*

ing their own well-timed jokes, weren't telling them any better than my grandpa. His stage was homier than theirs, but his audience was more adoring. Sitting at the head of their old kitchen table, extended with extra planks from the barn to stretch its length for the many mouths to feed, Grandpa held forth for his six boys and five girls, the oldest one eighteen years of age, the youngest one just two. From this table no one went to bed hungry. The pride that shone from Grandpa's eyes toward each of his children—the lengths to which he went, despite Sally's warnings about the dangers of pride, to "brag up" his boys and girls for their everyday accomplishments—filled his children's souls. The food could be scarce, but the love and the pride were not, nor was the laughter.

"I'd be willing to sell Sally if I could just get my price," Grandpa was heard to remark from time to time during the hardest of the depression years. "A million dollars an ounce!" Sally would just shake her head, her face pulled purposefully into a determined frown that never fully succeeded in pinching off the smile that played at the corners of her disapproving mouth.

The drama that played out before these children's eyes every day, Grandpa shouting or hugging, Grandma blushing or shushing, told them a powerful story. They had each come from love. Their lives were framed inside a story of the love of two others. Each child belonged to a greater bond that they had neither created nor could undo.

Grandpa and Grandma's love for each other had brought them into existence. Love so filled my grandparents' union that it spilled out from them in acts of procreative and nurturing generosity. The children were conceived in love. And they could each take as much of that love as they needed. There was more where it came from.

My mother remarks that she always knew she was loved, always felt secure in that love, always understood who she was because of that love. But it wasn't about her. She was about it. The love that framed her existence was not of her doing. She was of its doing. She didn't have to earn it. It had earned her.

Grandpa and Grandma loved each other. Their togetherness was the family's wealth. They were, simply put, *with* each other—not apart, not against, not above, not below—simply *with*. Hitch a carriage to such a powerful team of horses, let the little girl hold the strings, and she will really fly.

In contrast, Great-Grandpa Solomon reminds me of too many fathers and mothers today. They aren't around. In some respects, Solomon's parentage is to be preferred to the sheer absence of many fathers and mothers. The creator of my Grandpa existed. His drunken rages could be battled. Something was there.

Better this than the nothingness from which many children fear they come. From nothing, for nothing, to nothing. Created outside of relationship, these children are uncontained. They are not *with* anybody, ergo they are *not* anybody.

My friend Bishop Donald Clay had a painful epiphany about this some years back. Kids raising kids had turned into kids killing kids. And why not? Their lives were not real. Whatever had created them could not be verified. They were not the spillover of a couple's loving wealth, and there was no account from which they could freely draw. They were just a debt to pay, no one had the funds, and the bank was closed.

For these kids, living was a daily act of attempted robbery, an effort to break into the vault and steal the things they needed. Their existence was entirely up to them. If they were going to make it, they'd have to pull the heist alone.

Bishop Clay realized that the kids killing each other in the street outside his church doors were his kids. They belonged to him. The killing was his fault, as it was the fault of a whole community that had recklessly drunk from life's fountain with no thought for the well.

Marshaling a group of men from his congregation to join him, Clay turned his schedule upside down in order to be where the kids were at night. What he learned was chilling.

On several occasions, Clay was literally in the middle of teenaged gunfights, bullets searing past his ears. On many more occasions he put his life in peril by walking into a house or a bar long abandoned by all adults. This time, it was the kids who wielded the butcher knives, heroin or crack cocaine or the simple drug of rage fueling their rampage.

"I'm willing to give my life for these kids," he once told a deacon who challenged the wisdom of what he was doing. "I'm willing to die for the kid who kills me."

Bishop Clay didn't make fast progress. But he kept going out, night after night, month after month, year after year. "Why are you here, doc?" the leader of one gang or another would ask him, pulling his jacket aside to reveal the gun he had tucked in his pants. "I'm here to tell you this is all my fault," Clay would answer. "I'm here because you're here. I want to be with you."

From that seemingly insignificant beginning—a beginning as small as the word *with*—an entire community is being reborn. Onetime gang leaders are in college. Local entrepreneurs are teaching former drug dealers how to build lasting businesses. Young men are paired up with older men to learn to be good husbands and fathers. A school for kindergarten through twelfth grade serves nearly two hundred of my city's poorest children with no public dollars, and is producing achievement scores rivaled only by the best academies of the country.

Asked recently to account for their school's incredible success, the headmaster, Elder Milton Raiford, credited the very high academic expectations. "Our children rise to the level of our expectations for them," he said, "and so we expect a lot."

I totally agree with the headmaster, though I think that many people would fail to grasp the depth of his point. It is not the expectation that elevates the child. What elevates the child is belonging to loving adults who are expectant.

It was Augustine of Hippo, in the early years of the fifth century, who gave the Christian church its first deep reflection on the nature of God's three-in-one character. While it is true that there is but one God, and that God is God "all by Himself," God has *never* been alone. Within God, Augustine proclaimed, personhood and companionship are indivisible; eternal existence and undying love are one and the same thing.

Having come upon this incredible truth, Augustine immediately grasped the implication; creation was not the desperate act of a lonely deity. "Let *us* make humankind in our image" was not the impulse of a God who longed for the experience of love and worship. We were not born into the world, like too many babies born to unloved adolescent girls, for the purpose of providing what our creator lacks.

To the marvelous contrary, God birthed us into our own eternal existence for the simple purpose of loving *us*. Deposited in the bank of God is a fund of love so flush from an eternity of compounding appreciation that it will never run out. We can take from this account all that we need, draw from it as much as we want, even spend it recklessly.

We can afford to love; that's the simplest way to say it. We can afford to go ahead and take the risk, to love with all our heart, lay everything on the line, go for total broke. Whatever we might lose by pouring ourselves out into this desperate world will be replenished, with interest. Risk it all, spend it all, lose it all. Go ahead! Then do it again.

But can a person actually do this and live? Surely such a course of action is not sensible, not something God actually expects us to go ahead and do. Wouldn't a small exercise in judicious reserve be advised? A little holding back, laying up, salting down? Wouldn't this be prudent, what with our survival to worry about and all?

Indeed! And this is the same weary protest we've been making since we started keeping time and score. Wouldn't it be prudent to hold back a little—maybe more than a little; maybe a lot, as a matter of fact—so as to ensure our survival? Who can blame such sensible reasoning? No one can! And no one does!

Except God. Our spend-it-all, give-it-all, risk-it-all God blames this reasoning. Hoard if you like, God tells us in so many inventive ways—manna that *had* to be eaten that day, talents that *had* to be reinvested. Hoard, if hoard you must! God says. But plan on a wretched and pitiable harvest of eternally unendurable corruption. "You'll have hell to pay" says it plainer.

My Grandpa's choices amaze me. If anyone could be forgiven for living stingily, he could. He started out in an unrecoverable deficit and suffered further compounding losses over a lifetime. The few promises made to him in his tender years were broken, and his rags never did turn to riches. Loss, insult, and heartbreak were lifetime companions, and try as he mightily did, he never lifted himself beyond subsistence.

And yet, my Grandpa lived large. He loved big. He gave all. He risked and tried and trusted, again and again and again. His children felt they were rich, knew they were loved, believed they were capable. Grandpa had nothing yet lived as though he could afford to give everything, and give he did.

This amazes me, for no one told Grandpa in his early years about a generous, loving God. As a matter of fact, no one told Grandpa about *any* kind of a God when he was a lovelorn boy, and his continuing hard life should have suggested to him that the universe was a mean, cold tyrant. No one explained to him that there was, in fact, plenty to go around, a universe of love about him, a magnificently full and big purpose for his life. Yet he knew these things, or better put, he made the choice to live as though these things were true. He chose to love, to risk, and to give; it is this choice—it's always a choice—that amazes me.

I say that Grandpa could be forgiven for living stingily—that is, if *anybody* could be forgiven for this choice. But in fact, nobody is excused for living small. No one gets a pass, whatever the circumstances of loss and sorrow and lack. Life isn't fair in this matter. We were born of love, born to love, no exceptions.

The young men in my city who choose to strike out in rage are not let off the hook, though their early sorrows are immense. And the many of us whose lives are comfortable—we who avoid our raging neighbors in fear for our own well-being—have no excuse, either. Indeed, though no one is excused, we are excused less. From those to whom much is given, much is required.

My Grandpa liked to laugh. Let me rephrase that: my Grandpa chose to laugh. He preferred a life filled with laughter to its alternative, and despite the reasons he justifiably might have applied to a life of bitter smallness, he chose—he courageously preferred—to laugh and love and live.

I adore him for this. He understood—somehow had grasped—the deeper truth about life's unfairness. We don't get what we deserve, don't receive what we earn, don't inherit what's coming to us. This is such excellent good news, for at best we deserve nothing, earn little, and have no real claims to anything. At best! At worst—let's be honest here!—we deserve the fetid fruit of our miserable choices and selfish preoccupations. But the good news—ah! the *good news*!—is that we *don't* get what we deserve. The thought of this is explanation enough for my Grandpa's laughter. God is merciful, oh blessed day! What we deserve, we do not receive!

But even better than this, what we actually end up getting from God is what we *don't* deserve. I'm betting that this is the bigger and happier joke that put my grandfather onto the floor, his body racked in spasms of laughter, his children splayed about him, arms and legs and little bodies akimbo, themselves delirious in the hilarity of their big, strong daddy reduced to gasps and snickers. Where had all this goodness come from! God is gracious, oh double-blessed day! What we do not deserve, we receive!

Indeed, where *does* all this goodness come from? Turning his pockets inside out like a beggar-clown, showing the holes that were bigger than his big fists, my grandfather's lifetime answer was this: "The goodness doesn't come from me!" Empty pockets, empty hands, happy smile, full heart—my grandfather understood the happy joke of existence: it's all a gift. Pain and sorrow and disappointment all stirred in, life and love come to us free for the taking, fully loaded, eternally rechargeable.

God made it so. And who can account for the choices of God? Does a carefree child account for the choices made by her parents? Not when it was love that birthed her, love that undergirds her universe still. When mom and dad loved each other at her conception, love each other in the unremarkable background of her daily play, and when they promise without note or fanfare to keep their pledge to always love, childhood is filled with peals of laughter.

And so is our universe. Grandpa tapped into what's most deeply true: God is love. Love never ends. We are a gift. Eternally rich and pleasurable life is offered to us totally and absolutely free of charge. God's got extra, and He likes to share.

Of course, we have some choices in the matter. Like the child who spurns his daddy's love, squandering every family-born advantage on selfish occupations, the child of God can likewise be a cad. As a matter of fact, we have the authority to be perfectly, ridiculously ungrateful, if we insist. The gifts God likes to share, we don't have to accept. He's no brute about this. And He's no pathetic ego, either, wringing His hands because He needs us to love Him back. Whether or not we receive what He offers is totally our decision. God is very grown up about this, very full within Himself, very clear about what love is, He being its author and essence. This thought makes me want to shout.

"Giddyap!" is the first expression that comes to mind. And can you think of a happier human utterance? The horses are mighty, they're born to run at a blinding synchronous speed, and we've been given the strings.

"Yes!" also comes to mind. "Yes! Please, God, take me with you! Without you, O God, I am utterly lost!"

# Chapter 3: God *With* Us

When Clarence pulled his tiny body over the railing of his crib, dropping inelegantly onto the bare pine floorboards of the cramped bedroom he shared with his parents and baby brother, nobody noticed. His mother was out gathering the eggs that would be the family's breakfast, and Esther, Gladys and Sam—six, five and four—were busy tugging on their heavily darned clothes in an adjacent bedroom for a day of simple chores their mother would try to make seem fun. Marlin, not yet one, didn't stir on the tiny mattress that Clarence had just deserted.

My grandpa and grandma were still young parents. Sally was pregnant with Ruth, though perhaps on this day she was not yet aware that her sixth had been conceived. The year was 1921, Grandma was twenty-five years old, and the great tragedies of her life had not yet struck, not the ones that would sharpen her daily vigilance and carve into her forehead the deep lines of anxiety that I would later come to know so well.

Grandpa had finished his barn chores, having wolfed a thick sandwich—home-cured ham on freshly baked bread—that Grandma made for him before dawn. He was gathering up his spades and burlap sacks just as Clarence pushed open the kitchen door. Grandpa didn't hear his twenty-one-month-old son's squeal of delight upon spying his daddy by the barn. Striding quickly across the newly mown field of hay to the stand of trees beyond, he didn't glance back and notice that Clarence, barefoot and wearing only his diaper, was hustling after him just as quickly as his pudgy, unsteady legs would go.

My Grandpa and Grandma's life was not easy. There were no days off, no unexpected windfalls, no lucky breaks. Grandpa's forty-acre farm was no prize, either. Its small rocky clearings sloped steeply up to the edge of Shade Mountain, making plowing difficult and impoverishing every year's scant harvest. Huckleberries, peaches, and apples added a few dollars to Grandpa's yearly take as the huckster of produce in nearby Cocolamus and McAlisterville. Butchered hogs, dressed chickens, and fresh eggs made a greater contribution, as did the seasonal potatoes and corn and squash and beans they shoehorned into every tillable spot of ground. Only much later would a small timbering and sawmill operation tip the Hepner economy from near destitution to basic sufficiency.

Even years later my mother, Mary, next in line to be born into this blessed family, remembers her Daddy struggling to find the "cash money" needed for his children's shoes. Resourceful as he was, some things could neither be grown nor built with his rough tools. Even on his long days of huckstering in town, during which he exchanged some basketsful of home-grown or home-cured food for the silver dimes, quarters, and sometimes dollars he received, Grandpa saved all he could. On those days lunch was a single egg, which he handed over the counter to be fried for him by the town diner's cook. The purchase of a cup of coffee legitimized this frugal exchange.

All this being true, Grandpa didn't complain. Whatever were
the true fears and burdens Grandpa that carried in his heart, his visible
behaviors were that of a man rising early each morning to move with
gusto—and often song—into his promising day.

This was one of those days. The potatoes were ready for digging,
and signs were that the sacks would be extra full this year. Much later in
the day, the facts would confirm that Clarence had successfully made his
way to the place where his daddy had cut from the field onto the logging
road that led from this mountainside farm north into the heart of Shade
Mountain. What Clarence failed to notice was that his daddy did not
remain on the mountainous pathway, but had departed the trail shortly
after disappearing into the trees so that he could locate the "back patch"
he'd filled with this year's planting of potatoes. Already further from
home than nearly anyone would later believe possible—or be inclined
to search—Clarence had doggedly stuck to the dark-shadowed trail, just
sure that his daddy must be around the next bend, or the next, or the one
after that.

What no one can fathom is what Clarence felt as he lost his way,
as the shadows darkened, as his body tired and failed, as he shifted
quickly from confidence in finding his daddy to the unspeakably large
feelings of terror and panic and despair, all held inside the small package of his little body. That he felt such things cannot be doubted. The
impossible distance of miles he covered suggests the agony that drove
him. And in the end, to leave the trail altogether! To finally veer deeply

into the tangle of brambles and sharp sticks and thicker forest with nothing on his back or his legs or his feet to protect him! The lacerations Sally would later inspect as she cradled him, bad enough on his thighs and calves, utterly terrible on his little feet, illustrated for his weeping mother the story he would never tell her of his journey into horror. Whatever *lost* signifies, Clarence fleshed out its fullest meaning. Whatever lost feels like, Clarence suffered its extremity.

What Clarence did not do was pioneer the experience. Being lost is the common denominator of our humanity; it is our deepest shared affliction. I might say it more strongly than this: to be lost is to *be* human. The condition of lost is part of the very design of us. I am human. I am lost. Lost am I.

There is a childish and petulant complaint that quickly rears its shortsighted head on this point. "But why should it be this way?" we whine. "How unkind of our creator—if there even is a creator—that we should exist as lost! If there's a God," we rail, "and if He's so totally strong and good as everyone claims, wouldn't such a God have made us found, created us finished and knowing and sure?"

Well, actually, no! The God who is, the God whose being is inseparable from strength and goodness, would do nothing of the kind. The God who creates us with self-awareness and personhood, with the seed of His very life sewn into our eternally living being, would not make us human and found. He would make us human and lost. He would, if His love for us was awesome, His plans for us breathtaking, our future overflowing with purpose and meaning. Lost is where we must start. It is, if we are to ever become useful and whole.

But I have gotten ahead of myself. Before we can draw any meaningful conclusions about the necessity of the human experience of lostness, we must address a matter that is more fundamental. It is fruitless to rush forward here into defending the God who sensibly equips us to have to blindly seek him in the woods—even, at times, to the very heart of despair—if we don't believe that there even is a God.

*Lost* begs a question. The question is, "From what?" There is no *lost* where there is nothing from which to be lost. If our existence is, fundamentally, a crazy fluke, an aberrant happenstance, then whatever place or condition we find ourselves in can serve as all the reference point we need. We cannot be lost—we certainly should have no reason to struggle with feelings of being lost—if we have come from nothing. How should the human soul even recognize oneself as *lost*, let alone inconsolably grieve its lonesome state, if we do not belong with someone?

It is not just the diapered twenty-one-month-old, utterly dependent upon the love of his mommy and daddy, who cannot tolerate *lost*. Clarence's desperation, his wantonly misguided and foolish clamber into abject darkness, reveals our human nature, not his childish nature. Men and women of all ages stagger into the woods every day, searching for they-don't-know-what, cutting themselves off from their survival provisions in various kinds of blind grope for something that matters more than survival. And what could matter more than survival. Relationship matters more. No longer being lost matters more.

*Lost* is the universally shared human experience that rumors the existence of that which has been lost. Someone has been lost. Someone with whom we should and must be found has been lost. Our true state as beings who were birthed out of relationship and also made for relationship has been lost.

A great problem arises here, however. Though created in relationship and for relationship, we don't actually know, lost as we are, what *relationship* is supposed to look like. Indeed, *relationship* may be the word that we most badly misuse, applying it, as we do, to any old kind of human connection that we make, both the life-giving ones and the abusive.

And so, none of us should cop a pose of judgment on this. Just why, indeed, would our maker arrange things such that *lost* and *human* go together? We ought to hold off posting our list of grievances on this subject, not knowing, as none of us do, how to achieve what we're after, let alone what it is in the first place.

So here we are again. Lost is where we must start if we are to ever become useful and whole; this is my claim. Lost is the necessary human condition that we must suffer in order to receive the gift that makes it all worthwhile.

Let's take a breath here. The questions that must now be answered, like a cliff-face which seems impossible to scale, require our full presence. Just exactly what is this gift that somehow makes it all worthwhile? And why is *lost* required for its gain? These are our timeless questions. "What?" "Why?" "What does God want?" "Why is God doing this to me?"

For starters—let's take it step by step here—if God wanted, say, mindless obedience, He could have arranged things differently than He has. Hardwired into our makeup could have been commandment and law and good old common sense, with an instinctual guidance system built in to assure that we just do the right thing.

Obviously, we can rule out *mindless obedience* from our list of "what God wants." He could have arranged for it but evidently didn't. *Obedience* He wants; it says so in the bible. But *mindless* can be scratched from our list. Are there any arguments on this point? Good luck trying to make them!

Well, then, how about *cowering worshippers*? God could have had cowering worshippers in spades, if He had wanted them. Simplistic acts of divine terror would have done it. Still would. A rip in the fabric of the cosmos through which He momentarily slips His hand—in the sight of all the world—and we'd be on our faces worshipping our maker with all the superstitious ardor of any fear-based religion known to ignorant man.

So much for *cowering worshippers*. God could have put us prostrate on the ground before Himself in an instant—all seven billion plus of us—but clearly hasn't worked His magic this way. Worship, He wants. Also in the bible. Cowering, apparently, also, not.

So, we rule out *mindless* and we rule out *cowering*. Good enough. And we're left with *obedient* and *worshipper*, which is reasonable. *Obedient* and *worshipper* seem like the kind of qualities your regular God would want.

But it's more involved than this. If we rule out *mindless*, we're introducing the quality that exists in its absence. Let's call it *thinking*. The absence of *mindless* is not an absence, after all. It's a presence of thought and perception and analysis and conclusion. The awful thing about *thinking* is how prone to being wrong it is. *Thinking* would be a dangerous business to want your human beings to get into, it seems to me. *Thinking* would also be a terrific challenge to pull off within humanity, at least and do it well. Indeed, I can't see that your average God would ever go for this, as your average religion doesn't, either.

And then there's *cowering*. Could God really want what the absence of *cowering* implies? Is *fearless* in His business model for humanity? Could it be that He is neither offended nor threatened by the prospect of His creatures becoming *fearless?*

If you were God—go ahead and try to imagine it—and if you wanted to create beings that would grow up into fearless, thinking persons, how would you pull that off? Even if you considered such a risky gambit, would you choose to fund it? Would you mortgage the house, stake your bank account on it, go for total broke? I hardly think *I* would.

Inarguable is the following.

Thinking for yourself, as opposed to safely regurgitating the thoughts of others, demands the capacity to be dangerously wrong. Wrong thoughts, which are inevitable in the course of learning how to think any thoughts, invariably lead to wrong conclusions. Wrong conclusions get you lost. It's not complicated. Personhood requires thinking. Thinking leads to lostness. To become human is to get lost. That's the deal.

It's all part of a bigger, wonderful package. Just as personhood requires lostness, growth requires failure. Learning requires screwing it up. You don't like the package? You want no screwups, no failures, no desperate nights in the dark of the woods? Then copy your neighbor's homework. Safely barricade yourself inside the unchanging routines that used to work. Toady up to someone who's more than willing to do your thinking for you.

Dodge the deal of your own humanity, if you think you must, and squeeze whatever comfort you may from the increasingly necessary delusion that you're always right, always successful, always found. It's your choice. God wants your personhood, and in favor of assuring that you may receive it, He allows you to abide in perfect self-deception, whatever the exercise may finally cost you.

God is a businessman. His enterprise is the creation and growth of eternally living, never-dying beings who may grow up into fearless, thinking persons of inestimable worth to the universe. And, well, there's a price to this business, as there's a price to any business. The part of the price that we pay is the price of sorrow and grief as we discover that the course we set took us astray. What a price of pain we bear when we realize that we've placed our own lives in absolute jeopardy and that we are beyond our own hope. What despair to realize that all is irredeemably lost. We reach this point, every one of us, this point where we cry out, "I am lost! Without you, O God, I am utterly lost!"

The part of the price that God pays in this business is the price of finding us. Nothing in His design for our humanity prevents him from going to His own extremity on our behalf. He chooses to allow us to lose ourselves as perfectly as we may, for the sake of our human-ity. God Himself pays the full price of this choice by chasing after us, however extreme our flight, for the sake of His divinity. Love demands this of love, which is the same thing as saying that God demands this of Himself, and He freely and unendingly gives it. It's His bargain, and He keeps it.

Nearly one hundred searchers combed the yard, searched the barn, fanned out across the fields, and even walked great patches of the woodlands in close human chains around Grandpa's farm in search for Clarence. They did it again and again, hour after hour, morning turning into afternoon, and afternoon into early evening.

They considered the well, the depths of which could not be fath-omed and which would have been an instant death if he'd managed to tumble in. They considered the raging creek, which was swollen from the heavy rains the night before and had the strength to take a toddler anywhere, wedge him under any of hundreds of embankments, pull him into distant parts, larger rivers, God only knew. They considered the cougar, which still actively roamed Shade Mountain and was frequently spotted by one farmer or another.

What they did not consider was Clarence's capacity to simply walk up into the mountain, to turn his face into the darkness of the trees and to climb away from his home, from his mother, from his breakfast, and from the whole world that he knew. By early evening, the search-ers were exhausted and in despair, finding it ever more maddening to



*With: A True Story*

execute new search strategies as the young mother looked at them with imploring grief and the young father bellowed desperate recommendations, charging off again and again into futility.

Several times that day Layman Leister suggested that they hike up the mountain, which was patently ludicrous. And so as afternoon turned to evening and the team of searchers became increasingly impotent, Layman set off by himself. No one had dashed after Clarence's daddy more energetically and loyally all day long than this neighboring farmer. No one was more drained and grieved than he. But off he went, nonetheless, pursuing one more fool's errand, his solo search a mere needle stab into the immanity of a monstrous wilderness. He went alone, for it was in his nature and his need to go regardless what the others thought of him or of his folly.

Layman hiked a mile, his breath quick from the strain, the shadows darkening. Clarence could not have come this far! Layman hiked a second mile, the air beginning to chill. There was no point, but he could not stop. In the third mile, a rain-soaked patch of pathway revealed three toddler's footprints, and Layman's soul became a torch of need and purpose. It was darkening quickly, and running back down the mountain for help would ruin the light that was left. And so, alone, he ran, shouting Clarence's name, crying out to God, wiping his eyes, gasping for air, and willing himself to scrape the uttermost of his being to continue.

Layman could never adequately convey the improbability of what happened next. As he ran, as he wiped his tears, as he cried out, his eye caught a mere fleck of white, seventy yards off the trail, a thicket nearly obscuring all sightlines. He saw a fleck, or thought he saw it, and off the trail he careened, the darkness settling around him. Branches and thorn bushes and brambles whipped him as he pushed to the spot, rounded a large tree and found Clarence–asleep and shivering and bleeding and balled up like an infant in the womb, his diapered behind jutting up in the air to serve as the signal flare for help which had summoned Layman to his rescue.

"Found!" Layman bellowed, wrapping Clarence within his farmer's massive arms as he ran back down the now-moonlit mountain. "Found!" he yelled, summoning whatever was left of his soul. Every eight or ten paces, far too far away to be heard, Layman could not stop himself from repeating his refrain in an effort to get a word back to the grieving and desperate mother and father that their lost son was found. "Found!" he yelled. And "Found!" and "Found!" and "Found!" and "Found!" and "Found!"

When at last Sally heard him, anything and everything that can possibly be imagined changed forever. Mother and father and neighbors and children ran madly toward the distant peels of good news coming out of the mountain, as Layman ran and shouted madly toward the cries and shrieks that told him it was finished.

And then it was just Layman and Sally, for it was she who reached her savior first, she who wrenched Clarence from his arms into her desperate own.

I asked everybody who could possibly have known to please describe to me this scene of Sally receiving back into her arms the son who had been lost, the son who was not dead, not drowned, not swept away, not torn apart by animals, not cowering alone in terror in the dark of God-knows-where. Only one account of this moment survives, and I doubt that there was ever any other, it being too sacred and too intimate a scene for decent people to want to speak of.

"You . . . should . . . have . . . seen . . . that!" These words were spoken by the quiet-mannered Jake Lauver to his wife, Mary Emma, later that evening, and she then passed this same spare account on to others, it being so utterly adequate. My uncle Sam passed Jake's words on to me, the words spoken slowly and strongly in the same manner they had been conveyed to him. "You . . . should . . . have . . . seen . . . that!"

My uncle Hep—Clarence's nick-name picked up later in his boyhood—had no memory of his ordeal. He never spoke of it, hadn't the words with which to tell. Hep was a man of very few words even after he acquired more. What I remember is his stillness, the thankfulness that always shone in his eyes, and the glint of life's wonder.

One other thing changed forever that night on Shade Mountain, and that was my grandmother Sally's relationship with Layman Leister. Sam also told me this. "She'd finish a fresh batch of apple butter, and while the crocks were still cooling, she'd be down the road with one for Layman. Same when she dressed chickens or smoked bacon or picked huckleberries. Nothing was too good for Layman, no gift too extravagant." A thoughtful pause came here in Samuel's recitation of the story. And then he looked up at me, an almost startled look on his weathered face as he considered something that had just occurred to him.

"I think mother would have given Layman her very life if he'd have asked her for it," Sam then said, his old eyes staring into a distance. "Given him anything . . . and done it gladly."

# Chapter 4: Us *With* Us

"The man takes the drink. Then the drink takes the drink. Then the drink takes the man."

Grandpa Hepner warned his boys about this. The terrible ghost of alcohol haunted him for many years. Believing that the best defense is a good offense, he threw himself full-bodied into his life with Sally, with his brood of children, and with the daily battle to scrape a livelihood off the side of a mountain that spent the whole of his energy every day.

Grandpa warned his first three-pack of boys about alcohol's power, having watched his own strong daddy become enslaved by its whips and chains. Once, when grandpa was not quite twenty, he took a single shot of whiskey, the only alcohol to ever touch his tongue throughout his lifetime. For weeks afterward, Grandpa could think of nothing else but that terrible taste that he needed to taste again. This cautionary tale was repeatedly told first to Samuel, Clarence, and Marlin, and then in due course to all the generations of boys since, including my brothers and me and likely, too, my ten male cousins and their several dozen sons and grandsons.

"The man takes the drink." That's where it always begins, Grandpa told his boys. A choice is made. The man lifts the cup to his lips and he drinks. Grandpa's warning shot worked its way down into the soul of his

<hr>

children—the boys in the direct line of fire, the girls collaterally—and in both good and bad ways, his story of the irresistible cup took effect.

Grandpa didn't direct his warnings to his daughters straight on, or at least there is no account that he did. Esther and Gladys were his first-born, both of them demure and virtuous. Esther grew up and married a man who illustrated her daddy's concerns about alcohol quite colorfully. Gladys, more sensibly, steered herself entirely clear of the liquor-weak gender.

Samuel, Clarence, and Marlin were followed by Ruth, Mary, and Ferne, who in turn were followed by Dick, Donald, and Kenneth. In each of the eleven, the war against alcohol was waged: life was pitted against death, wakefulness against slumber, sobriety against the alluring numbness found at the bottom of several kinds of bottle. Battles were won and lost; there were casualties, as there always are; and for the vast most part, the children of my Grandpa and Grandma eventually came out as heroes, battle scars and all.

Perhaps to acknowledge the reality that each of his children would have to choose from among several life courses, Grandpa equipped them each with several names. Esther was Dinky Dear, among other things. Gladys was Hardy, Sam was Rosey as well as Timothy, Clarence was Hep, and Marlin was Jobie. Ruth was Tasslie, Ferne was Findley Frankhauser and also Findley Friction Tape, and my mother, Mary, was Tiddlebaddley as well as Scagey. Dick was Harriet Louise, and apparently none the worse for it. Donald was Jim, or perhaps Jim was Donald: I have quite lost track. And the youngest, Kenneth, pulled the shortest straw in the nickname business as youngest children are prone to do: Kenneth was Baboon Baby.

"The man takes the drink," Grandpa told them. And when they each became men, they proved him right. Samuel, Clarence, and Marlin started drinking during the war. Marlin had followed his big brother out from his mother's pacifist church to serve, along with Sam, in the brutal foxholes of Europe. Clarence, having totally satisfied any appetite he once had for adventure, stayed behind on the farm and simply slipped behind the barn to serve his time in the bottle. Dick, heading up the second three-pack of boys, shipped to the Pacific, where he did most of his drinking below deck. Ruth's husband "drank responsibly," as they put it, for he was wired to be able to handle his duties as well as his liquor. Only my mother married a Mennonite boy, and he knew better than to try to sneak a drink anywhere but on the fishing boats of his non-Mennonite friends, where he was safely shielded from the prying eyes of his community. Ferne, like her big sister Gladys, took the prudent route of singlehood.

Not for a second do I blame my Grandpa for the almost superstitious sense of alcohol's power that he insinuated deep into the imaginations of his offspring. Alcohol was the destroyer of anything and everything that might have been his childhood. He witnessed his daddy's near-lifetime of enslavement up close, as well as his mommy's, for it was a fact that "poor, old Fianna," as he later referred to her, never saw that she had any other choices but to wring her hands, to remain at great peril with Solomon, and to offer her empty promises to her boy. "You be a good boy and keep yourself free of that liquor," she frequently in-structed my Grandpa during his childhood and early teenage years, "and I'll buy you a gold watch!" From his tenderest years, Grandpa knew that she was never going to buy him that watch. He knew it just as clearly as he knew that she, too, was a slave to drink, even if she wasn't the drinker.

And so I hold no blame at all against my grandpa for the near reverence—of the fear-based kind—that he instilled in his children for alcohol. There is no special box upon which I can stand to judge him for the role he played in perpetuating alcohol's grip. I can't imagine that I'd have done any differently or any better, had his life been mine, and the far greater likelihood is that I wouldn't have done as well.

Which changes nothing of the facts. Grandpa's children fell for drink, or for drinkers. And within the tableau of his one person, both the man who displayed the daily courage for wide-awake living, and the child who feared the lurking temptations of numbness and unending sleep, Grandpa embodied the fundamental choices of human existence. It's not a question of *whether* you drink, Grandpa's life declared. It's a question of *what* you drink. Cup of life or cup of death. Cup of wonder or cup of slumber. Drink the rich draft of living and take into yourself all of life's nuances of bitterness and sweetness and pain and pleasure, just as the appreciative connoisseur takes in the complexity of aroma and taste found in the skillful vintner's barrel. Or drink the imitator's cup, the one that turns down the sound, dims out the lights, and blurs over all that's real and true about our pain-racked and precious life.

"The man takes the drink," Grandpa taught. And so does the woman. We drink to life or we drink to death. We lift the cup that is our own life and drink it fully into ourselves, or we push the cup of our life away, refusing its taste in favor of one that slowly alleviates the experience of having to taste anything at all.

When it comes to our own experience with our own experience, the choice could not be easier to express. Just reviewing the previous few sentences, the point is made. The oppositional prepositions of *down* and *up* and *out* and *over* and *away* stand in perfect contrast to the relational prepositions *into* and *with*. Do we have the courage, as Grandpa had the courage, to receive *into* our own lives all that is our own life— to be *with* ourselves? Or must we push ourselves away to a sufficiently dimmed-out distance so that we don't have to suffer the brightness of being the being that we are?

This battle—will we embrace or will we reject our humanity?— has raged for two thousand years over the humanity of Jesus. Every heresy of note since the death and resurrection of Jesus, simply put, has been an effort to sever His divinity from His humanity. With a level of determination and creativity that ought to strike us as quite suspicious, group after group has arisen in these two millennia to announce that Jesus "only appeared" to suffer (since God could not, Him being God and all, suffer!) or that He was not actually God, since the fact that He *did* suffer proves it. These efforts—claiming that He was not human! that He was not God!—share the purpose of denying the fullness of life, inclusive of life's suffering.

In point of fact, our view of Jesus' humanity—how real was it?—
is the fulcrum upon which our lives tilt, either toward our own greater
fullness or in the opposite direction. It is an urgent matter, it seems to
me, for all who may consider receiving Christ's life into their own life
to have some understanding about the quality of that life that they are
electing to receive.

There is a terrible scandal wrapped up in the story of Jesus—
indeed, there is a very good reason to put big-time distance between
ourselves and the life of God offered to us by Jesus. The scandal of
receiving Jesus' life, like the scandal of receiving our own, requires
courageous and grown-up manhood and womanhood, my Grandpa and
Grandma's kind, the kind that is willing to accept the suffering that is
stirred into full human living rather than to insist on its narcotization.

It was into precisely this story, the one about our human suffering
and the irresistible cup of drunken slumber, that Jesus was born a
human, helpless, skin-and-bones baby. God became flesh, which I
would never have advised. Jesus Himself declared that He came so
that we can be way more alive, which many of us quail to consider.
He shared His life with us, and by all accounts He allowed himself to
taste what is pleasurable and delightful about living. He also took an
unprecedented pounding, suffering to the uttermost of human suffering.

The night before He was executed, Jesus prayed to His daddy
to take away the cup that He'd been asked to drink. This, now, I can
appreciate. The most understandable of all acts is the act of pushing
away the cup of our own life. Jesus begs for a pass, as we all beg for a

pass, but then He yields to the one who knows better, agrees to drink it all up, and speaks those famous words, "I won't do what I want, God. I'll do what *you* want!"

What Jesus was willing to fully experience is precisely what we are unwilling to fully experience. It is no great mystery to me why we push him away. We don't want to suffer as Jesus suffered. We don't want to lose what Jesus lost. We don't want to die the way He died. We don't want to live or to love the way He lived and loved, and herein is the crux—the cross—of the matter.

God is the maker of life and of love. He forges the life we each now experience for no other purpose than love: that He may love us; that we may love each other; that we may love Him. To live and to love—to possess and to be conscious of our God-natured and love-natured being—comes at a price. God's love nature is not stingy. His love for us includes His desire for our personhood, which makes room for our rejection of Him and His gifts. Forged in His image, our living and loving is also of this same roomy kind, which means that we too will love at times without being loved back, will give without always receiving, will be alive in ways that at times cause our suffering. This is the life deal. If you don't like this deal, then pronounce martial law and try as you might to squat squarely on top of anything that moves. If that exercise sounds too exhausting, liquor will help you pass the time.

As God is the maker of life and love, God is also the maker of marriage. Jesus himself loved a good wedding, and in one notable instance, He supplied its festivities with the best wine of the evening. If

Jesus had appeared on the slopes of Shade Mountain in 1911, when my Grandpa and Grandma were celebrating the start of their long and full marriage with all the ardor and appetite of the young, Jesus would have figured a way to further enliven the event. On that particular occasion, He would surely have known better than to symbolize His approval of their passion with the gift of good wine, but whatever miracle He'd have gift wrapped for this party would have made the same point. Jesus, like His daddy, approves of the party that is our human life.

Indeed, Jesus approves of the complete deal of human existence. When He took His own turn within the bounds of human experience, He considered it entirely worthwhile. He responded in the affirmative to the mixed conditions of His own life, just as my grandparents responded affirmatively to the mixed conditions of their life, its richer and poorer, its better and worse, its sickness and health. When He, like they, was asked to declare whether He promised to keep His vows to the life He had embraced, He shouted a most resolute "I do!" And in His "I do!" He triumphed over the fear that sorely tempted Him to say "I do not!" which would have led Him, as it so often leads us, to a limitation of Himself, a limitation of those around Him, a limitation of life's risks as well as its potentiality. Jesus drank the life cup to the dregs, and He rejected the irresistible cup of slumber, numbness, and death.

If we ever really came to terms with Jesus' humanity—No one was ever more alive than He!—then we would know that He is pointing us to a fuller embrace of our own humanity. Our Lord says, "Be more alive!" Our world and we with it say, "Be less alive! It's neater."

"The man takes the drink," my Grandpa taught. "Then the drink takes the drink. Then the drink takes the man." First, he warned of it, and then it came to pass.

Sam, Clarence, and Marlin descended into heavy drinking and into dimmed and diminished living. Sam and Marlin both had plenty of painful things to deal with, painful things they were going to need to fully feel if they chose to remain alive.

Sam returned from war to discover that his beloved and beautiful wife had placed herself into the arms and beds of other men within days of having said goodbye to him. She had no remorse about this fact nor the slightest interest in the marriage that to her had never been for real. Marlin was deeply wounded in both body and soul by being one of the few survivors of a trench massacre of such inhumanity that he struggled for many years with feelings of envy for the dead. A year in a military hospital in England was required for the doctors to piece him together well enough to ship his ghostlike self back home to his parents. And then there was Clarence, who just fell into the drink without any particular provocation; he neither fought his way into the bottle, nor had any fight inside of himself to get back out again, either.

For Sam, Clarence, and Marlin, the drink had taken over and was doing the drinking. My Grandpa and Grandma watched helplessly as the drink then began to take over the lives of the men who were their firstborn sons.

"I had no will to stop," Sam shared with me. "Just like Pop said, I took one taste of it, and that was that."

Clarence, too, was a hopeless case. "Once Hepper got his first bottle, he was gone." My mother's the narrator here. "If you wanted to find Hep, you'd have to go behind the barn and pull him down off the woodpile."

As for Marlin, it was sadder. The waif of a ghost who quietly slipped back into his parent's home after the war made no scenes about anything. Uncle Jobie did his drinking in his room, and no one had the heart to challenge the things that he did to survive the nightmare that had become his life.

From the start, I have narrated the story as it occurred and as it was told to me by my mother and by her ten siblings. Over the course of nearly fifty years, I had the pleasure and privilege of talking at length with each of my mother's siblings, from Gladys at the top of the line to Ken at the bottom. I cannot count the nights I slept at Gladys's house nor the nights at Ruth's. I cannot with any adequacy convey the aroma and the taste of endless meals with Hep's clan, thanks to the remarkable cooking of his wife, Molly. Or the equally remarkable meals dished out by Esther or by Jim's wife, Julia.

And though my Grandparents were greatly subdued by advanced age during my boyhood, gatherings in their home stretched on for days at a time, everybody pitching in with the food and the festivities. On those occasions I spent precious times with Sam and Jobie, for Grandpa and Grandma's house was their house, too. Both of them jumped up at the end of every meal that I can remember, reached into their pockets, and passed out silver dimes and quarters to my cousins and me "for eatin' real good." You can pretty well bet that I was paying attention to anything and everything that went on around me throughout those many years.

I recount this long shared history to try to convey just how in the thick of these memorable people's lives I have lived for so many rich years, how many were the eyewitnesses who recounted these tales to me, how well corroborated were their stories. Nothing of this effort changes the fact that the miracles I am about to report require an exercise in belief to receive them as true. Miracles are like this: they occur so surprisingly within the realm of what is too ordinary and commonplace for the miraculous. Yet miracle—the intrusion into the realm of the possible by that which is impossible—does occur, and my uncles' stories of destruction became the stage for the miraculous.

Samuel, Clarence, and Marlin stopped their drinking cold and in the very same way. They each turned from the cup of death to the cup of life without a backward glance. They each reported, and then demonstrated through the rest of their long lifetimes, that alcohol had lost any and all allure.

Sam, Clarence, and Marlin, each in their turn and at their own time, asked for the life of Jesus Christ to take over their own lives. When they each did this, their drinking stopped immediately and permanently.

Their pain didn't diminish, nor did their losses vanish, nor their wounds or fears or sorrows. The flesh of Sam's flesh did not repent of her promiscuous ways and return to him, nor did the flesh of Jobie's

flesh miraculously restore itself to the places on his body from which
it had been torn. Their life was hard, as before, and their nights lonely.
But they no longer needed the cup that deadened them to their lives.
They didn't need the drink that helped them forget what they felt. They
replaced that cup of dying with one of living, receiving into themselves
the life that God both offered them and offered to share with them.

"The man takes the drink," Grandpa had told them. In the course
of time, my uncles turned their back on the family's thirst for alcohol
and its promise of annihilation and turned their face toward their
father's fully grown-up embrace of the better cup that was their lives.

It's not such a bad thing, really, this full living of the life we've
been given. It has its compensations, after all. For one, when we choose
to remain alive to our own sadness and suffering, we also remain alive
to our joy and our bliss. It's one package. Numb out the pain and we
numb out the pleasure. Allow our hearts to shatter and break, and we get
bigger hearts.

And the maker of all things is always right there with us, too.
That's no small consolation. He totally knows what it's like to be a
feeling human being, Him having been one too, so His company is of
the encouraging and cheering-up sort.

There are the truly tough times, of course. No news here. There
are the times when all we can manage to do is breathe. Women have
such times, for example, in undergoing childbirth, breathing and
suffering through until there's a baby. Both women and men have
these times in their 3:00 a.m. attacks of panic or loneliness or despair,

breathing and suffering through until there's a dawn. At these times prayer can get stripped bare. "O God," may be all we have the presence of soul to moan, or more simply, just "God!" or simpler still, "Oh!"

So, the cup that is our living can really deliver a mean kick from time to time. But what a drink it is, what a draft of rich, full, precious living! It brings tears to my eyes, the brightness of its taste and the warmth of the burn that it leaves. So raise your glass with me! Thank God for the cup that is your life and lift it to your thirsting mouth. And then, please, drink!

To life!

# Chapter 5: Us *With* God

Grandpa and Grandma were *farmers*; that states it simply. Their business was their farm, and the purpose of their business was the care and growth of their children. This is easy enough to state, but it's not so easy to explain, and it was not at all easy—it actually was complex and difficult—for them to have actually been all of the things that the little word *farmer* includes.

For starters, there was the care of the land itself. Grandpa's forty acres was divided roughly in half between what was tillable and what wasn't. The tillable ground, most of it sloped rather than flat, needed to be plowed each spring, then harrowed and raked, and then planted.

Horses were required for this work, or mules, and at different times Grandpa had a pair of both. So the tiller of ground was also a *horseman*, or a *muleteer*, as the case may be. Either way, the husbanding of large work animals isn't something one picks up over a weekend; their nutrition, foot care, treatment of diseases, and compassionate handling are advanced arts and skills handed down from generations.

Throw in *machinist*, for the plow, harrow, rake and planter required machinist's tools and skills. Parts broke, and the poor farmer either was his own *toolmaker*, or he watched his crops fail.

*Safeguarding the seed stock* was essential; would you know

how to do that job? What conditions keep seed corn fertile through the winter months? Oat seed? Wheat? And how would you do the math to assure that you're only consuming what you can afford to consume—especially when every human, animal, and bird you feed is hungry right now—and that you're holding back enough for next year's planting?

The challenge of taking on all the vermin and pests could fill its own library, and the reading of the weather was a daily preoccupation. *Exterminator* and w*eatherman* must join our list. Timing each harvest for maximum yield required a precarious balancing act between the factual matter of whether the crop was totally ripe and the prognosticative matter of whether the threatening storm would turn the oats you cut that morning into sodden mold. Just as impossible to predict were the occasional locust incursions that would beat you to the harvest, simply eating the wheat field to the nub right ahead of your scythe. May as well put s*eer* and o*racle* on the list of job titles.

And we have not even begun to fill out our list. There was a cow, for the family needed milk: *herdsman*. My mother found the job of minding the cow the single most boring and hateful assignment of her childhood, and yet it had to be done, for the hayfield was not fenced off from the crop of oats, and while the imbecilic cow was allowed in the hay, she far preferred the oats.

Chickens give you eggs, but not magically, so you needed to be a *poultryman*. Grandpa kept the birds that had bright red combs on their heads, for he knew they were healthy. He killed those among his egg layers that displayed a paler color, sacrificing the eggs they might still have laid for the meat his family could immediately eat. He knew that these birds were weaker and more likely to die, in which case he would lose both the eggs and the meat.

One of the primary protein sources in the Hepner clan, apart from the daily eggs, was "the other white meat." Beef cattle were not an economical converter of feed to protein, not like the pig. So, add *pig farmer* to the list, and right behind it, *butcher*. The newly butchered pork, ribs, and fresh sausage went into large, well-scrubbed metal tubs, and straight to town for sale. Now add *salesman* to the list, too. Grandpa kept the bacon and the hams, cured them in a salt-and-vinegar brine, and then smoked them for several days over just the right combination of ash and hickory wood chips for the best of wood-smoked tastes. The ham and the bacon stayed in the family or was shared with Layman Leister; that treat was too special to sell off to strangers.

The other main source of year-round protein was venison, and in the Fall there was also rabbit, squirrel, pheasant, and turkey. Add *marksman*, too, for Grandpa surely was that. Bullets could not be wasted, and Grandpa was famous for his careful, clean, single-shot deadliness with the rifle, a quality picked up by more than one of his sons.

Some of the meat was canned; the boiling kettle of mason jars was a nearly constant fixture in Grandma's primitive kitchen from early July into late October. She canned beans, applesauce, peaches, cherries, sauerkraut, pickles—sweet and sour, bread-and-butter, and dill—and also corn, though corn was mysteriously difficult to keep. Time after time, Grandma would climb slowly out of the basement with a jar of corn that had lost its seal and "turned." Her face was a study in sadness and remorse for the awful waste she had regrettably permitted.

The root cellar was for potatoes, apples, and the crocks Sally used to store her apple butter. The apple-butter crocks were tied off with a piece of cheesecloth, and usually Sally needed to knife off a thick layer of mold when she opened a fresh crock in the winter months; no matter in this case, since mold was as an excellent seal against spoilage for apple butter.

Apples came up the root cellar stairs every night, for it was Grandpa's custom to take up his vocation as *storyteller*, sitting at the table long after the evening meal was finished, as Ruth and Mary were laboring through their daily chore of washing dishes. The other children crowded about the table with homework, mending, or play. This was their favorite time, storytime, which Grandpa was the master of. His audience ever rapt as he told them of exciting, unsavory, and—by virtue of the perspective he took in the retelling—hilarious dangers he survived as a child. Sally quietly glared her disapproval at the telling of these tales, for she did not believe that children should know about or be exposed to such unmentionable things, and she certainly didn't see the prudence in making these dark affairs seem exciting or funny.

Grandpa told his tales every evening while the sharp blade of his pocketknife peeled, cored, and quartered apple after apple. As he carried forth his narrative, he systematically doled out the apple quarters to each of his eleven children in order, youngest to oldest, piercing each thick



*With: A True Story*

slice on the point of his knife's blade and holding it out toward the next child in line. His stories cycled around and around his long and well-loved play-list, as the apples cycled around and around his kitchen full of children, until everyone had received their happy fill.

We have not spoken of the half of Grandpa's land that was not tillable but rather covered by woods. Over time, Grandpa saw an opportunity to turn this unproductive acreage into a small timbering business. He had saved enough money to purchase a motor and blade strong enough to turn his trees into ten-by-ten-inch ties for the railroad. From this small start, Grandpa branched out into timbering other people's forest tracts. His fourth-grade education notwithstanding, he became well-known in the whole of Hiester Valley for his ability to walk through a several-acre stand of old trees, wrap his arms around each mature trunk, train his eye up its length, and from this homespun methodology estimate precisely the tens of thousands of board feet of lumber he would subsequently pull from his saw blade. *Lumberman, estimator, sawyer,* and, again, *salesman* join the list, and for seizing upon an opportunity that no one else had seen, add *entrepreneur.*

We have also not spoken of the *carpenter* that Grandpa needed to be, or the *baker* that Grandma was, kneading her great mounds of dough twice each week for the dozens of loaves of bread she coaxed perfectly out of her wood-fired cooktop only to see it devoured, often still hot, like cotton candy by her six boys. My eighty-four-year-old mother still often speaks of this, how hard her mother worked on the bread, how the boys would tear off great pieces, slathering them with apple butter, and inhaling them without seeming to give their mother a second thought. And we've also missed *washerwoman* and *auto mechanic* and *seamstress* and *motivational expert*! But the point is made.

While my grandparents' business was farming, the skills, resources, knowledge, planning, and commitment required to conduct their business was many dimensioned. The purpose of their business was the care and growth of their family, and this care and growth involved both providing for their children and, ever so important, engaging their children in the very same work that they did. After all, children are neither like wards of the state nor like hired hands. They must pitch in themselves, and whatever might be gained through the shared labor of a family is as much their own gain as it is their parents.

This pattern fits the universal one. We must know what business we are in; we need to know the answer to that question very clearly. We need to put our assets and our skills to the service of making a success of our business. We must calculate the cost of the investment that is required. We must make a plan and devise a system to measure our progress against our plan toward the outcome we seek. We must exercise the will to face the surprises and the setbacks that will come.

And most important, we must know what our ultimate purpose is. What is all this for? Are we going about the work merely for its own sake, or are we stewarding the work that we do in such a way that it contributes to the care and growth of others? Does our business venture both provide for the needs of others as well as engage them as partners and participants in the work that we do?

Grandpa was a businessman, and I say that the pattern of his business fits the universal one, but I must explain myself on this point. Time was when business was *always* for something other than business. That's the "universal pattern" of which I speak. Time was when there was always a purpose in business that was bigger and greater than the business itself. Until lately in the human story, business *always* served the care and growth of people, in most cases those people being the family members of the business owner. Business was the strategy and means used to achieve the purpose of the business. Business served people, not the other way around.

Did the family business owner—farmer or butcher or marksman or cook—fire the son or daughter who at ten or eleven or twelve years of age broke the plate she was drying? Let's get our heads clear on this point. Business was for people. Business served a greater goal than itself, and that greater goal was always the care and the growth of others. The enterprise could in no wise be called a success if the people it existed to serve did not, in the course of time, themselves become the masters and the owners of the work that others had done before them, and which would be carried on by still others after them, too.

This "universal pattern" derives from the originator of all patterns. God is, after all, the pioneer of business, as God was the first entrepreneur. God, like my Grandfather after him, works with a patch of ground, some areas of it more obviously tillable and fecund than others. He has a purpose, for which He marshals His resources and makes His investments. His purpose, as we have already discussed, is to bring into being eternally living, never-dying persons who may grow up into powerful, fearless, and capable God-companions, fellow workers on the farm of God, stakeholders in their daddy's world-building, people-loving, story-telling enterprise.

A time comes in the lives of many a son or daughter of God when all that's been invested in us just "clicks." The love and companionship we've been offered from the very beginning of our tender years adds up to a conclusion, on one or another wondrous day, that fizzes up and over the rim of our self-preoccupation. We were created in love, sought out by love, offered companionship in the daily joys and sorrows of love, and invited to roll up our sleeves and to make our own contribution to the ongoing work of love.

We are someone: that's the short of it. We are someone because of *the* someone who has popped the cap off the bottle of His own life for the singular joy of sharing His favorite taste with us.

What finally "clicks" is that we've been created for the purpose of joining the company of God in a most incredible business, yet not just of joining, but also of becoming coinheritors. This business of God is an enterprise of such extraordinary dimension. We can glimpse just how extraordinary it is precisely because we get to spend some time being one of its products, on the way to our becoming one of its producers. To generously share our very life in creative and procreative feats of derring-do—now that's an enterprise you want to get in on! To both love and respect those around you so much that you provide them the true freedom to find that they are free indeed—would you like a piece of that action? To venture into wild and distant frontiers on the greatest treasure hunt on earth, the hunt for the human person who has gotten lost in searching for you and for the company you now joyfully keep— does that particular safari catch your imagination?

Like the children who grow up on family farms or in the woodworking or leatherworking or butchering or baking businesses of their moms and dads, Jesus grasped what His father was up to very quickly and eagerly got to work while He was still a child. The very first words spoken by Jesus that are recorded in the bible capture this moment. Jesus' parents took Him to the temple when He was twelve, and the entourage headed back toward Nazareth without Him, an easy enough mistake in an extended clan that did not require a child's mom and dad to constantly hover.

Two days out, discovering that Jesus was not in their company, Mary and Joseph raced back to Jerusalem in sheer panic, only to find their boy sitting among the scholars in the temple and teaching *them*! His stories and insights held the priests and clerics in rapt attention because though they knew the things He was telling them, His retelling of these ancient texts made them come alive. He spoke to them, as was often said of Him later, as one who "knows what He was talking about."

"How could you have put us through such terror by remaining here without telling us?" was essentially what Jesus' parents threw at him.

"Didn't you know," Jesus answered, "that I would have to be

about the affairs of my father's business?"

And in case it occurs to someone to protest that twelve years old is cruelly young to expect a child to get to work, let me point out that when it is mom and dad you are working with, it's not a violation of child labor laws. Just try to stop my uncle Sam at the age of twelve from taking his own turn behind his daddy's horses as the field was readied for planting! Just try to stop my mother Mary at the age of eleven from taking scissors to cloth and cutting out the pattern that would be the new dress her mommy was showing her how to make. When we're working with the one we love and admire, we haven't the patience to wait to try the work out for ourselves; we want to show that we can do it, to create and produce the very same thing that our mom or dad takes great pride in creating and producing every day.

Jesus picked up this theme in his adult ministry with his disciples: "I know, now, that the things I've told you and shown you have finally clicked," Jesus exclaimed. "You're ready, now, to do the things that I do, to love others the way I've loved you—not because you're told to do it, but because it's now inside of you. Therefore, let's have no more talk of being servants or clock-punchers! You're owners now, friends! You're family, and that means that we're in this business together!"

My Grandpa was a farmer, an entrepreneur, and a teller of tales. Conceived in his likeness and raised to share in the affairs of his family line, so am I. My city is my farm; I've always thought of her this way. The fields I look after and the fencerows and tree lines I traverse are different from his, but these things are only particulars. I

have Grandpa's farmer's view. This ground I till, these neighborhoods
and streets and enterprises and vexations with which I relate each day,
will become my children's inheritance. Like every farmer, I know that
the soil I handle must be enriched. It doesn't exist for my sole and
immediate service. Farmers till their ground in perpetual awareness of
the fact that their children and grandchildren will reap the harvest of
their work. Their children will and their neighbor's children with them.
Foolish is the farmer who only thinks of this year's crop!

I also inherited my Grandpa's attraction to opportunity; I think
that says it nicely. I take risks, more plainly stated. I see potential where
others don't. Some of the time, I see potential where there isn't any.
That's the risk.

And, oh, the thing for which I am most deeply grateful: I love
stories. Truth be told, I need stories. I listen in rapture to well-told
tales, and in their absence I try my very best to craft some—because
a good story well told makes all the difference. "Man cannot live by
bread alone," Jesus once said. We need words, and the more the words
are straight from the mouth of God—true in their telling, good in their
report, big in their consequence, and loving in their character—the
more they are life itself. This isn't whimsy. Our very existence and
the existence of everything we conceive of as reality is created and
continually sustained by God's enrapturing power with words.
So, what Grandpa was, I am too. I am, because of the God who made
my Grandpa and then saw fit to put me in his line.

Earlier I said that no one told my Grandpa in his early years about a generous and loving God, that no one told Grandpa about *any* kind of a God when he was a lovelorn boy. But he learned. He learned from the bible stories he read, from the tent preachers he went to hear, and then from the young, shy, believing girl who was fully glad to accept a bid for marriage from a man whom no one else considered fit.

Ah, yes. The entrepreneur passes down to me through more than one line! Sally, too, was a risk-taker and an investor in long shots. "She's my *Beema*!" Grandpa often said. A preacher had told him that the *Beema* was the Jewish seat of judgment which, oh grace of grace, was transformed through Christ into the seat of mercy. Grandpa knew about such turns of fortune, about good things coming to him that he didn't deserve. Grandpa understood the gamble that his wife had taken on him, and he lovingly addressed his wife as *"Beema."* Of all the nicknames he bestowed on those he loved, *Beema* was the one he used the most. The risky bet that Sally had placed on him, pushing all her chips into the center of the table on a terribly shaky hand, gave my grandpa all the daily reminder he needed of the salvage operation God was conducting on his behalf.

So, it's an extended-family deal. It is for each of us. We pick up the lines we've been given, God as the giver, our parents or aunts and uncles or grandparents or teachers or mentors passing on the gift that they, too, were given. We're becoming like God, is the thing that must be said. We're not becoming God; let's not be ridiculous. God is God and God will always be God. We are not God and never will be God.

But because of who God is, because of His bigness toward us, we

are invited into His likeness. We're His children, after all. His business
is becoming our business. What He does, we will increasingly do. We're
growing up.

As I grow older, I gain a stronger and stronger fellow feeling
for my Grandpa. I often wonder if the delighted feelings that I feel as
stories pour out from within me are like the feelings he must have felt
as he peeled and quartered his bowl of apples, passing them around the
table along with his stories to his hungry children. And in this work
there is a likeness also to God's work, for He is a storyteller, too. Our
efforts, my Grandpa's and mine, are far paler, to be sure. But in each
one of our efforts there can be a likeness to the very work of God. His
bigness toward us makes this so. We, too, can stitch together a saving
tale, and like the girl who makes her first dress, its lines crooked and its
seams erratic, we are encouraged by our loving maker to practice our
inadequate stitching and then to go ahead and put on what we've made
and wear it to town.

The inadequacy of our effort is not what God calls attention to.
The flubbed line, the dropped stitch—these things don't interest God.
"Look!" He says. "See my daughter's pretty dress? She made it! Listen
to my son's story! Isn't it good?"

It's our growth that God is interested in, and so He patiently
corrects us again and again, cheers us on, and brags us up. "You're
growing," He encouragingly points out. There's a universe of creative
and restorative work ahead, and His plan, His pleasure, is to let us help.

# Chapter 6: Me *With* Sam

Sam and I spoke many times throughout each year of my adult life, exchanged notes and letters, and visited whenever possible. He became a dear friend to my wife, Milonica, and quickly befriended my daughters, Emma and Clara. On one occasion, Sam made the trip in my direction, packing his weekend clothes into the smallest, most tattered suitcase I have ever seen in the hands of a grown-up, its diminutive size hardly seeming capable of holding the clothes of a doll.

With each phone call, with every visit, I observed the steady and unmistakable decline of my uncle and my friend. He shrank as I grew. He became quieter as my life became noisier. He slowed and thinned and retreated further and further into the stillness and solitariness of himself.

In what turned out to be my last visit with Uncle Sam, I arranged to drive from my home in Pittsburgh east to Lancaster to pick up my then-eighty-one-year-old mother so that she and I could drive together to visit with Sam in his home in Pennsylvania's Juniata County. I had already begun to pen the first pages of this book, and took the completed first chapter along, the one telling of my horse-and-carriage ride with him forty years back.

As was his custom, Sam was standing by the door when we pulled up. I was struck by how small and frail he had become, by the worried and slightly puzzled brow that framed the weathered and now also withered face from which his hungry eyes shown and on which his tentative, almost shy smile lay.

We ate a simple meal of toasted cheese sandwiches and tomato soup that I prepared, sitting at his small kitchen table beneath a replica of a painting Sam had inherited from my Grandpa, a portrait of an elderly man seated before a simple meal of bread and soup, his hands clasped in prayer, his eyes closed.

Retiring to the rocking chairs Sam kept in his kitchen, I asked him if he would do me the favor of listening to a new story I had just begun to write, a story about him.

Sam's face registered confusion and uncertainty, as though he had not heard me clearly or was unsure what the individual words in my sentence added up to as a whole. "He wrote a story about you, Sam!" my mother repeated to him, her voice loud, her words imbued with significance.

Sam's eyebrows registered astonishment, his face, delight. Any prospect of a good story was welcome news to my uncle, and to have one written about himself! If I had told him he just won the lottery, his face would not have registered a greater boon.

I read to my uncle slowly, my voice steady, my eyes glancing up again and again to make sure that I was keeping his pace, that I was not losing him, that I was with him. The memories I was sharing with him were over forty years old; I had never shared them with anyone before, and their accuracy was a point of anxiety for me, as was their candor concerning the choices Sam had made in his youth.

We had switched places. I was now forty-seven years old, just the age Sam had been when I clambered up beside him on his carriage that long-ago day. And he now sat before me as a child, his face glad and trusting, his eyes needy and insecure.

I read of his time in the military and of his divorce, and Sam's eyes lowered to the frail and almost translucent hands he held in his lap. I read of the wondrous carriage ride, and his eyes rose up to meet mine, a look of faraway wonder on his face. I read of my dejection after arriving back at his house, this very house, and Sam's eyes glanced over toward my mother, a look of regret and sorrow taking hold of his brow in just the same way that I had so often seen regret and sorrow take hold of my Grandmother's brow.

Then I read of the movie about bank robbers, and Sam's face went blank. His gaze turned inward as though he had stopped listening or needed to consider matters apart from what I was narrating to him.

The only clue that Sam was still with me was the quick glance I saw him make toward his refrigerator when I read of the Coca-Cola we had drunk together. While I read about little prepositions and about the particular one that is the greatest of all, Sam's face remained burdened, his eyes turned inward, his gaze unfocused except for the several additional times he glanced toward his refrigerator as though it held an answer to a question that was troubling him.

I rounded in on the end of the chapter, finally reading its last lines. "So why don't you head to the fridge or the coffeepot or the teakettle," I read, "and set yourself up with a nice companionable beverage? Let's take a ride together, shall we? Pull a little heist. Share some time in the hoosegow. Are ya wit' me?"

The silence of the room moved in, then, to fill the space that had been occupied by my narrative.

Sam's gaze returned to the present, his eyes to me. And then a light of joy and relief bloomed on his face. "It was Zero!" he announced, his face a study in happy resolve. My mother and I glanced at each other. It was our turn to be puzzled and, if truth be told in my own case, disappointed.

"It wasn't Cagney," Sam pressed on. "The robber was played by Zero. 'Are ya wit' me, babe?'" Sam then joyfully repeated, bad-guy accent just as I had remembered it, even if my mind had plugged the wrong actor into his story. "I'm wit' cha!" he continued, his face as fully animated as I had ever seen it, the light in his eyes bright as he gave my tale back to me yet again, repeating for his own pleasure its happy lines.

"Zero Mostel and his buddies wanted the money from this bank," Sam then added. "But they didn't know about some Mexicans who wanted it, too." He was transformed, these new details pouring out of him with a freshness of energy that belied the four decades separating him from his night at the movies. "And after they robbed the bank, the Mexicans robbed them, and, oh!" Sam's face was radiant with the old memories. "It was all a big mess!" he concluded, chuckling.

"Kim Novak was something else in there, too," Sam then added, his head shaking back and forth at this additional memory, a sheepish grin on his face. I saw Sam's eyes once again glance toward his refrigerator.

"You don't happen to have any Coca-Cola in there, do you, Sam?" I then inquired. The look I received back from my uncle told me that this was his own question exactly, and that he surely hoped the answer was "Yes!"

I went across Sam's kitchen, the same one he had crossed on my behalf many years before, opened the refrigerator door, and spied a full liter of Coke. Gone were the sparkling glass bottles of my childhood memory. Gone were the cases of bottles of Coke that Sam stored in his cool basement to make sure he never ran out. Gone was the throng of noisy cousins, the living room full of loud, talkative, animated aunts and uncles. Esther and Gladys, Sam's older sisters, were dead, their proficient bustle around their mother's kitchen now a haunting absence. Clarence and Marlin, Sam's next younger brothers, were also dead, their soulful, silent owl-like vigilance now missing from this room, and I the poorer for it.

But Sam was still here with my mother and me, at least in this moment, and with two clean glasses retrieved from the back of his neglected cupboard—my mother demurely declined, never having acquired a liking for carbonation—I rejoined my old friend in our rockers, handing him a freshly fizzing glass of darkly caramelized soda.

Sam took a drink, his eyes immediately tearing as the bite and the burn hit his nose and throat, or as the memories of life's treasures refreshed themselves in the taste of his favorite beverage, or perhaps as he considered the words he was preparing to say.

He took another sip, turned his head left and right in satisfaction, and then looked at me, his old face warm, his eyes rheumy.

"I sure like your story, John!" Sam said the words in his slow, strong way, his face proud, his eyes sincere. "How you could put those words like you did!" he continued, his head shaking in wonder. "Where did you learn that?!"

It wasn't a question. It was Sam's way of giving special emphasis to his recitation of praise, his manner of bragging about yet another one of his remarkable nephews and nieces, praise that each one of us has been lavished with, by Sam assuredly, if not also by our own Hepner parent. After all, Sam learned this way of bragging up the younger ones from his own parents, as did each of Sam's brothers and sisters.

Where did I learn this business of shaping words into a story?! Sam's question overjoyed me with the ludicrousness of it. "I learned to do this from you, Sam!" I said loudly, my heart so very glad. "I learned to do this by spending time with you!"

Indeed, I learned to put words to the service of a good story from my Uncle Sam, and from my mother, and from my Uncle Dick, and from the whole brood of Hepners, including my older cousins Terry and Kenny and Doug as well as my eldest brother, Tom, to name a few. Sam and his brothers and sisters learned it from their father, and back the line it goes to the father of the very greatest story of all, the one about love that surrounds each one of us, chases after us, wraps us into its massive arms, and grows us up into its very likeness.

"Can I hear the rest of your story when it's finished?" Sam then asked. The question was meant to underscore his pleasure in what I had done and in me.

Sam died a few months after my mother and I visited with him. He died nearly a year before I wrote another word of this story. I don't believe for a second that this means that he hasn't heard the rest of it.

In the end, Sam's death came quickly. The hundreds of family and friends who later gathered for his funeral could each have told a powerful story of how their soul had grown because of Sam's way of paying attention to them. Those who were children when they first met Sam could have told of the double portion that was their blessing in knowing him. Our souls became larger because Sam was able to close the gap between his own bigness and our smallness; even though we were small, Sam was truly with us.

Only a few staff at the nursing home where Sam had been taken were present when he quickly and unexpectedly slipped away; a cousin was among them. In the moments before my Uncle Samuel breathed his final breath, his eyes flew wide open in glad astonishment, his face brightening into that amazed and also shy smile that conveyed his lifetime habit of deep appreciation for whatever goodness he received. Sam was radiant as he gazed toward what only he could see.

"Look!" he effused in his slow, strong way. "Now they're coming for *me*!"

John Stahl-Wert (www.johnstahlwert.com) is the President and CEO of Pittsburgh Leadership Foundation (www.plf.org), a "fourth-sector" agency with thirty years of strategic investments in the transformation of the culture of Pittsburgh. He is coauthor of the international bestseller *The Serving Leader* (San Francisco: Berrett-Koehler Publishers, 2003; www.theservingleader.com) and *Ten Thousand Horses* (San Francisco: Berrett-Koehler Publishers, 2007; www.tenthousandhorses.com), both written with his friend Ken Jennings. He is married to Milonica Stahl-Wert, an artist, and is the father of two daughters, Emma Elizabeth and Clara Ruth. John is at work writing *For*, the second of three books in the *With* trilogy.

The cover design and artwork for *With* was done by Philip E. Greene, Jr., Creative Director of Expanding Minds Creatives. Expanding Minds Creatives, (EMC) is a multi-disciplined design studio based in Pittsburgh, PA. EMC provides visual and industrial design solutions in conjunction with marketing expertise. EMC engages corporate and social organizations alike. Additionally EMC is dedicated to providing opportunities for young creatives to work along side of working professionals through personalized mentorship. For more information concerning EMC, please call 412-916-0673.

To learn more about *With: A True Story*, listen free-of-charge to several chapters of the audiobook version, narrated by the author, view photos of the characters in these stories, or follow the progress of *With's* sequel, visit:

# www.WithATrueStory.com

# www.WithATrueStory.com

CD Audiobook of With narrated by the author

Companion Study Guide